ENGINEERING CHALLENGES

BUILDING ROCKETS

by Rebecca Rowell

D1706953

FOCUS READERS

WWW.FOCUSREADERS.COM

Focus Readers is distributed by North Star Editions:
sales@northstareditions.com | 888-417-0195

Produced for Focus Readers by Red Line Editorial.

Content Consultant: James Flaten, PhD, Associate Director of NASA's Minnesota Space Grant Consortium and Contract Associate Professor in the Aerospace Engineering and Mechanics Department at the University of Minnesota – Twin Cities

Photographs ©: 3DSculptor/iStockphoto, cover, 1; Indian Space Research Organization/AP Images, 4–5; MSFC/NASA, 7; Lori Losey/KSC/NASA, 9; Bill Ingalls/HQ/NASA, 10–11, 15; Randy Beaudoin/KSC/NASA, 13; KSC/NASA, 16; Victor Zelentsov/JSC/NASA, 18–19; Aubrey Gemignani/NASA, 21; SpaceX, 23; Red Line Editorial, 24–25, 27, 29

ISBN
978-1-63517-255-3 (hardcover)
978-1-63517-320-8 (paperback)
978-1-63517-450-2 (ebook pdf)
978-1-63517-385-7 (hosted ebook)

Library of Congress Control Number: 2017935926

Printed in the United States of America
Mankato, MN
June, 2017

ABOUT THE AUTHOR

Rebecca Rowell has worked on numerous books for young readers as an author and as an editor. Her writing includes titles about ancient India, Rachel Carson, John F. Kennedy, and the Louisiana Purchase. Rebecca has a master's degree in publishing and writing from Emerson College. She lives in Minneapolis, Minnesota.

TABLE OF CONTENTS

CHAPTER 1

A RECORD-BREAKING LAUNCH

The rocket stood on a launch pad in India. Engineers watched with hope and a bit of anxiety. Six countries were involved in the mission. The project involved great risks. This rocket would be releasing **satellites** into outer space. But it would do so while traveling 17,000 miles per hour (27,400 km/h).

An Indian rocket launches to send more than 100 satellites into outer space.

The rocket was launched into outer space on February 14, 2017. It released one satellite. Then it released the others, one after the other. It took 18 minutes. Finally, all 104 were sent into outer space. It was a success! This mission carried the most satellites ever on a single rocket.

A rocket is an object that moves through the sky as a result of burning **combustible** material. As the material burns, gases shoot from the back of the rocket at high speed. This creates a strong force. It pushes the rocket forward.

A rocket is often shaped like a cylinder with a pointed nose cone. But rockets come in many shapes and sizes. A simple

A drawing shows an early Chinese rocket.

homemade rocket can be a few inches long and made with a few items. A space rocket has computers and many electrical parts. Some are several hundred feet tall.

The Chinese created the earliest known rockets in the 1200s. These rockets were likely used for war. The rockets had tubes of gunpowder attached to sticks.

Lighting the gunpowder made it burn. The **exhaust** launched the rocket into the air.

Modern rocketry is much more complex. In 1942, Germany launched the V-2. This rocket was able to go to outer space. However, the V-2 was instead used as a missile. It was flown horizontally toward a target rather than vertically toward outer space.

The next step was to actually send rockets to outer space. A rocket engine has its own oxygen supply. This allows it to work in outer space, which doesn't have oxygen. Rockets began sending satellites into low-Earth orbit in the late 1950s.

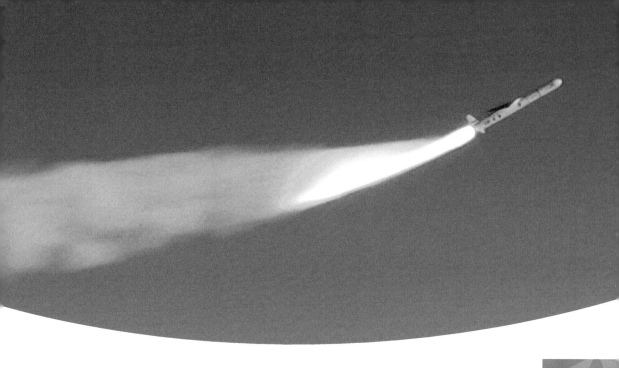

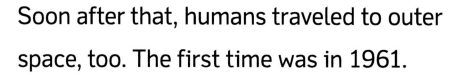

A NASA rocket flies toward outer space.

Soon after that, humans traveled to outer space, too. The first time was in 1961.

Today, engineers work to create better and better space rockets. These vehicles send people into outer space. They also launch spacecraft that explore our solar system. Rockets make these scientific missions possible.

CHAPTER 2

DESIGNING ROCKETS

Engineers design the three main parts of a space rocket. The first is the rocket's body. It must be made of material that is both strong and lightweight. The second part is the **payload**. This depends on the mission. The payload might be a telescope. It might be satellites. Or it might even include people.

A rocket must move fast to reach outer space and stay in orbit.

Engineers also design the guidance system. It is the "brain" of the rocket. The system can have a variety of parts. These can include computers, radar, sensors, and communication equipment.

Many forces affect a rocket in flight. Engineers designing a rocket must consider all of these. Thrust moves a rocket forward. Weight results from **gravity**. It pulls the rocket toward Earth. **Drag** also acts on a rocket. It tries to slow the rocket down. Drag acts on an object moving through the air. But there is no air in outer space. That means drag no longer acts on a rocket once it leaves Earth's atmosphere.

Workers install the payload fairing (protective cover) on the NuSTAR spacecraft.

Engineers consider the rocket's power, weight, speed of exhaust, and length of the mission. A rocket needs enough thrust to lift off and enough horizontal speed to orbit Earth. It also needs enough fuel to accomplish its mission.

Escaping Earth's atmosphere takes a lot of speed. A rocket must reach a speed of 5 miles per second (8 km per second) to stay in orbit. And it must go even faster to escape Earth's gravitational pull. This requires a huge amount of **propellant**.

Fuel and oxygen are mixed to burn as propellant. They make rocket engines work. They also make up most of a rocket's **mass** before launch. But eventually the fuel is gone. This makes the rocket lighter. It also means some equipment is no longer needed. The rocket can get rid of fuel tanks, fuel pumps, and even engines. This makes the rocket even lighter.

The Soyuz TMA-18 burns its propellant.

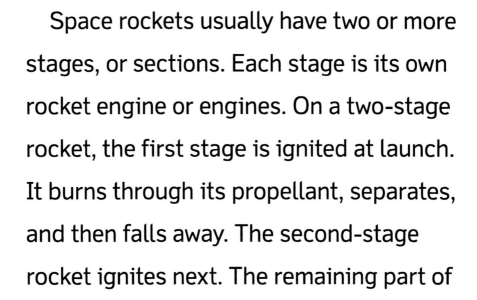

Space rockets usually have two or more stages, or sections. Each stage is its own rocket engine or engines. On a two-stage rocket, the first stage is ignited at launch. It burns through its propellant, separates, and then falls away. The second-stage rocket ignites next. The remaining part of the rocket goes even faster.

Space Shuttle Atlantis lifts off from Kennedy Space Center in Florida.

As engineers work, they must also think about cost. One rocket can cost millions of dollars to create. Engineers work to develop a rocket that meets a mission's needs and stays within a budget.

ENGINEERING DESIGN PROCESS

Engineers use special tools in their planning. Then they test their systems. Once a rocket is built, they expect it will work as planned.

ASK: What is the purpose of the rocket? How far must it travel? How heavy will its payload be?

IMAGINE: Look at other rockets for ideas. What type of rocket would work best? What failed in other launches? How can those problems be avoided?

PLAN: Draw a diagram of the rocket. Make a list of materials needed. Write down the steps to build it.

CREATE: Follow the plan and build a rocket. Models can help show how rockets work. Test the rocket model by launching it.

IMPROVE: Did the rocket fly as expected in a test launch? Did it reach its target? Change the design to make the rocket fly farther. Test it out!

CHAPTER 3

SOYUZ-U ROCKET

A Russian spacecraft was launched on December 1, 2016. The three-stage Soyuz-U rocket was unmanned. It was meant to carry supplies to the International Space Station (ISS). If all went as planned, it would arrive at the ISS on December 3. But even with great planning, things can go wrong.

A crew member admires a model of a Soyuz rocket.

Things did not go as planned. The rocket malfunctioned 120 miles (193 km) in the air. Much of the spacecraft and its cargo burned up in the atmosphere. The remaining pieces crashed in a mountainous area of Russia.

Engineers discovered that the problem occurred in the third stage. A pump connected to that stage's oxygen tank failed. The tank broke into small parts. This caused an explosion. Engineers think this was due to a construction error.

Russia responded to the investigation. First, engineers rescheduled the next mission planned for that type of rocket. They also changed the type of rocket for

A Soyuz rocket prepares for launch.

that mission. That meant Russia would not use up the last of its Soyuz-U rockets. In addition, Russia's space agency set out to determine if the same problem existed in its remaining Soyuz-U rockets. If so, engineers could fix it.

LANDING ROCKETS ON A SHIP

Most rocket stages are destroyed during launch. But a company known as SpaceX designed a first-stage rocket that can be reused. This is possible because the stage completes a vertical landing. It does so once it has finished propelling the second stage.

On April 8, 2016, a two-stage Falcon 9 rocket was launched. It was set to deliver a shipment to the ISS. After separation, the first stage flipped around. This was so it could enter the atmosphere backward. Next, its engines burned to slow it down. The rocket stage then landed gently on a ship waiting near the Florida coast. This was the first time a rocket stage had landed vertically on a ship. The landing was SpaceX's second successful vertical landing of a reusable first-stage rocket.

SpaceX's Falcon 9 rocket can complete a vertical landing.

A single-use rocket can cost more than $60 million. Launching a Falcon 9 repeatedly would cost only $200,000 for fuel plus some replacement parts. The ongoing success of the Falcon 9 reusable rocket stage could save millions of dollars every flight.

CHAPTER 4

BUILD A ROCKET

You've learned about rockets that can reach outer space. But rockets can be used on much smaller missions. For this challenge, you'll build a rocket that reaches a target on the other side of the room. Use a balloon and two straws to create the rocket. Then launch it so it flies to the target.

You can create a simple rocket using a balloon, two straws, and tape.

Materials:

To create the rocket, you'll need a balloon and two straws. One straw should be slightly wider. The other straw should fit inside it. You'll also need tape and a target. The target can be as simple as a piece of paper with an X drawn on it.

Procedure:

1. First, build your power source. Insert the narrow straw into the neck of the balloon. Tape the balloon to the straw so air can't escape when you blow it up.

2. Next, create your rocket using the wide straw. Seal one end of the wide straw by folding over the tip and

The air in the balloon will propel the rocket.

taping it down. Add paper fins to the side of the rocket if you like.

3. Blow into the narrow straw to inflate the balloon. Then pinch the base of the straw to keep the air in place.

4. Next, place the wide straw over the narrow straw.

5. Stand a few feet from the target. Aim your balloon in the direction of the target. Finally, release the pinch to let out the air and launch your rocket.

Improve It!

- What happened? Did your rocket reach the target? Did it fall to the ground? Did it fly straight? Make adjustments for your second launch.

- Vary the amount of air you blow into the balloon. For a better comparison, use the same angle for each launch.

- Try a bigger balloon and see how far you can launch your rocket.

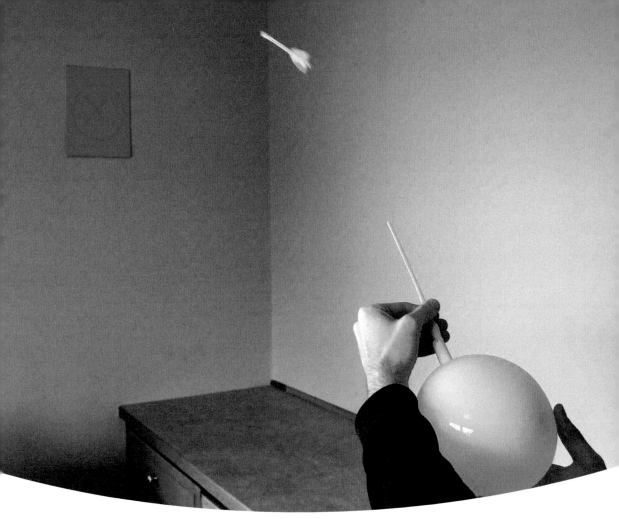

This rocket soars toward its target.

- Add a payload, such as paperclips. Remember, you'll have to adjust the power to make up for the added weight of the payload.

FOCUS ON
BUILDING ROCKETS

Write your answers on a separate piece of paper.

1. Write a letter to a friend describing what you learned about the December 2016 Soyuz-U rocket launch.

2. Rockets can be used for different purposes. Which one do you find most interesting? Why?

3. What does drag do to a rocket as it travels through the air?

    A. It pushes the rocket forward.
    B. It makes the rocket spin.
    C. It slows the rocket down.

4. When launching a rocket, what happens if thrust is increased?

    A. The rocket's fuel lasts longer.
    B. The rocket picks up speed more quickly.
    C. The rocket will slow down.

Answer key on page 32.

GLOSSARY

combustible
Able to be burned easily.

drag
A force that opposes motion.

exhaust
Used gas or vapor that comes out of an engine.

gravity
The natural force that pulls objects toward Earth.

mass
The amount of matter, or material, in something.

payload
The goods carried by a vehicle that are separate from the vehicle and not required for it to function.

propellant
A fuel plus a chemical to provide the oxygen that a rocket engine needs.

satellites
Objects or vehicles that orbit Earth, the moon, or another body in space.

TO LEARN MORE

BOOKS

Roby, Cynthia. *Building Aircraft and Spacecraft: Aerospace Engineers.* New York: PowerKids Press, 2016.

Schertle, Rick, and James Floyd Kelly. *Planes, Gliders, and Paper Rockets.* San Francisco: Maker Media, 2016.

Skurzynski, Gloria. *This Is Rocket Science: True Stories of the Risk-Taking Scientists Who Figure Out Ways to Explore beyond Earth.* Washington, DC: National Geographic, 2010.

NOTE TO EDUCATORS

Visit **www.focusreaders.com** to find lesson plans, activities, links, and other resources related to this title.

INDEX

Answer Key: **1.** Answers will vary; **2.** Answers will vary; **3.** C; **4.** B